CARELESS

Philippa Bateman

RISING STARS

Beth was talking to Lee on her webcam.
"I'm hoping Dad will be here soon," sighed Beth.
"But he's so forgetful sometimes."

3

"He'll be here," said Lee, trying to be helpful.
"Your dad's not thoughtless," said Roo butting
in. "He's the coolest DJ ever. Anyway, pity me!
Mum and Dad are out and Lee thinks she's the
queen of the world!"

"Pity you?" said Lee. "Do something useful and put the popcorn in the microwave!"
"I'll do it but only because you're useless ... Your Highness!" said Roo. He felt resentful because Lee was being bossy.

"Hey! You've got popcorn too," said Beth. "I'll come over and stay until your dad comes," said Lee. "Roo can bring some popcorn for us."
"Great, thanks!" said Beth, feeling a bit more cheerful.

Brad arrived soon after Lee.
He shouted, "Hi, Beth!" and
started rapping at the door.

Brad gave Beth and Lee a big high five each. "Why does he have to act like a DJ all the time?" thought Beth as she let him in.

Roo was glad Lee had gone to Beth's flat.

"If Lee was here now she'd be nagging, 'careful this, careful that.' Only two minutes," said Roo to himself, as he put the popcorn in the microwave. "I'll put it on for five minutes and then all the corn will be popped. No hard bits left!"

He pressed the button and went back to the webcam.

Roo saw Brad on the screen.

What's up, Brad?

"I'm buzzing, Roo. How are you?" said Brad, winking.

"I'm SWEET! I'm-a-top-hip-hop-popping-to-the-beat," rapped Roo.

Everyone laughed. Suddenly Roo scrunched his nose. There was a strong burning smell.

"Oh no, the popcorn is burning!" he yelled. Roo darted to the kitchen. There were flames in the microwave. He froze and was speechless with fear.

In a second, Brad and the girls had raced to the flat. The door was locked. Roo had the only key!

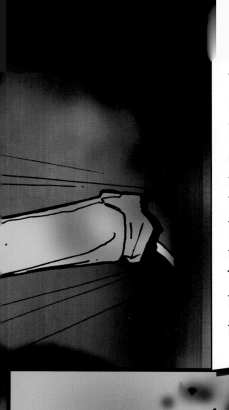

With a fearful look on his face, Brad kicked open the door. He dived over to Roo and pushed him to safety. Brad pulled out the microwave plug. The flames licked his hands, but he ignored the pain.

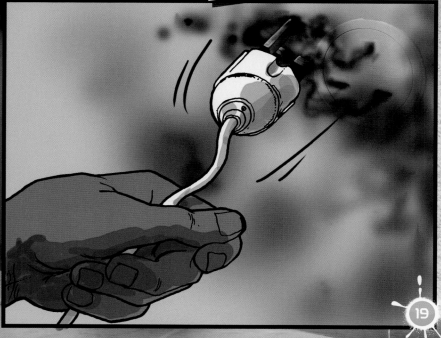

Roo grabbed the fire extinguisher from the wall and put out the fire.
"Is it really painful?" asked Beth, looking tearful.
Brad turned the cold tap on and held his hands under the cold water.